Ubu and the
Truth Commission

UBU and the Truth Commission

JANE TAYLOR

from the production by
William Kentridge and
The Handspring Puppet Company

UCT
PRESS

University of Cape Town Press

University of Cape Town Press (Pty) Ltd
University of Cape Town
P/B Rondebosch
7701 Cape Town
South Africa

First published 1998
Reprinted 2004
© Jane Taylor
ISBN: 1 – 919713 – 16 – 6

Photographs by Ruphin Coudzer, Johannesburg
Design, layout and typesetting by Gavin Younge Studio, Cape Town

Printed and bound by Clyson Printers, Maitland 7405, Cape Town

CONTENTS

WRITER'S NOTE

Jane Taylor

Truths and Reconciliations

In early 1996, almost exactly two years after South Africa's first non-racial national election, the Truth and Reconciliation Commission (TRC) began its work. The Commission had a momentous mandate. It was to solicit South Africans who considered themselves as agents, victims or survivors of human rights violations perpetrated in the apartheid era, to testify before a national forum. The purposes of this process were various: to retrieve lost histories, to make reparation to those who had suffered, to provide amnesty for acts which were demonstrably political in purpose. One of the larger purposes of the Commission is to create a general context through which national reconciliation might be made possible.

What has engaged me as I have followed the Commission, is the way in which individual narratives come to stand for the larger national narrative. The stories of personal grief, loss, triumph and violation now stand as an account of South Africa's recent past. History and autobiography merge. This marks a significant shift, because in the past decades of popular resistance, personal suffering was eclipsed— subordinated to a larger project of mass liberation. Now, however, we hear in individual testimony the very private patterns of language and thought that structure memory and mourning. *Ubu and the Truth Commission* uses these circumstances as a starting point.

The origins of the project

Ubu and the Truth Commission had several points of origin, some arising out of the Handspring Puppet Company, other projects, and some from William Kentridge. I can only address here where the project began for me. In 1996 I initiated a series of cultural activities, *Fault Lines,* which was a programme of events including an art exhibition, poetry readings by writers from South Africa, Germany, Chile, Israel, Norway, the Netherlands, Portugal, Canada, Sudan and Zimbabwe on issues relating to questions of war crimes; reparation, memory and mourning; as well as an academic and arts conference; a student radio project; a community arts initiative, and a workshop for media covering the TRC. My purposes were multiple.

Primarily, I wanted to foreground the role that artists could play in facilitating debates around the Truth and Reconciliation Commission. Following the premise that artists habitually deal with issues of betrayal, sadism, masochism, memory, I felt that to ignore what the arts could bring to these processes, was to waste an extremely valuable resource. Further, it is my feeling that through the arts some of the difficult and potentially volatile questions, such as why we betray or abuse each other, could be addressed without destabilise the fragile legal and political process of the TRC itself.

Alfred Jarry and his Ubu

The beginnings of the original Ubu have attained the status of legend within French theatre culture. At the age of fifteen, in 1888, Alfred Jarry used a short satire written by his friend, Henri Morin, which depicted their science teacher as king of Poland. Jarry's piece was conceived as a play for marionettes. The first public performance in Paris of a reworked version, now the fully fledged *Ubu Roi*, took place some eight years later. The riot which broke out in the theatre after this performance is a stock element of Jarry biographia. It is, however, worth noting that neither of the sequel Ubu plays, *Ubu Cuckolded* and *Ubu Enchanted*, was performed during the writer's brief 34-year life.

Ubu Roi follows the political, military, and criminal exploits of the grandiose and rapacious Ubu, a kind of parodic Macbeth who, together with his wife, attempts to seize all power for himself. The central character is notorious for his infantile engagement with his world. Ubu inhabits a domain of greedy self-gratification. The play is full of scatological jokes, and the famous opening line of the play ('Merde!'/'Shit!') was no doubt part responsible for the vigour of French public response of the opening night. Ubu's weapons are a pshittasword and a pshittashook, and his sceptre is by tradition a lavatory brush, a stage prop which you will see appear in our production. Characters in the play are named, variously, MacNure, Pissweet and Pissale; and at one point Ubu thrusts his conscience down the toilet. There is a particular kind of pleasure for an audience watching these infantile attacks. Part of the satisfaction arises from the fact that in the burlesque mode which Jarry invents, there is no place for consequence. While Ubu may be relentless in his political aspirations, and brutal in his personal relations, he apparently has no measurable effect upon those who inhabit the farcical world which he creates around himself. He thus acts out our most childish rages and desires, in which we seek to gratify ourselves at all cost. It is this feature in particular which has informed our own production.

Ubu in South Africa

In *Ubu and the Truth Commission* I have taken this figure, and have characterized him using a style of burlesque derived in part from Jarry. The language is in ways deliberately archaic in order to situate Ubu as an anachronism, a figure who lives within a world of remote forms and meanings. This character is then placed within a new dispensation, the world of the Truth and Reconciliation Commission in South Africa.

Rather than represent any particular figure from South African history, Ubu stands for an aspect, a tendency, an excuse. Nonetheless, he does at times speak in voices reminiscent of those we have heard in South Africa during the TRC hearings. I have then set his linguistic world against the languages arising from the actual testimony which has emerged out of the Truth and Reconciliation process. The testimony is drawn from the hearings which have given us access to the stories of both survivors and perpetrators of atrocities committed during the Apartheid era. Over the past eighteen months of listening to the disjuncture between the testimony of those looking for amnesty and those seeking reparation, it has been chilling to note the frequency with which an act of astonishing cruelty has been undertaken, as it were, negligently, with no sense of the impact of such actions on other human lives; when confronted with the families of victims or survivors, those perpetrators who seem to have some capacity for remorse, appear to be shocked at observing, as if from the outside, the effect of their behaviour. Others simply show no response at all, so profound is the denial, or the failure of moral imagination. Our purpose, in this play, was to take the Ubu-character out of the burlesque context, and place him within a domain in which actions do have consequences. The archaic and artificial language which Ubu uses, with its rhymes, its puns, its bombast and its profanities, is set against the detailed and careful descriptions of the witness accounts which have been, in large measure, transcribed from TRC hearings. Ubu is confronted within his own home by those whom he has assaulted.

It is as if Cause and Effect are registered through different modes of expression in the play; this carries through into the performance styles which have been used.

This structure, of Ubu meeting the TRC, gives our play its meaning. Obviously, there are very specific theatrical results. Perhaps most evidently, we are automatically taking on the burden of the farcical genre which Jarry used. I remember having lengthy debates, with a student, about the ethics of Charlie Chaplin's *The Great Dictator*, and whether one could ever explore human rights abuses through a burlesque idiom. My responses now are perhaps more complex than they were then. The TRC is unquestionably a monumental process, the consequences of which will take years to unravel. For all its pervasive weight, however, it infiltrates our culture asymmetrically, unevenly across multiple sectors. Its place in small rural communities, for example, when it establishes itself in a local church hall, and absorbs substantial numbers of the population, is very different from its situation in large urban centres, where its presence is marginalised by other social and economic activities.

Much of the information that most of us receive on the TRC is communicated via the media, between commercial slots, sit-coms, magazine programmes, and so forth. We are called upon to respond with outrage, sympathy, or wonder, within a context that inculcates bewilderment and dislocation. Given our information overload, it is not so easy to sustain unambiguous feelings of moral outrage, even while we might sustain internal sensation of indeterminate sadness. There is thus, I suppose, a sense of ambiguity produced by the play. This is not an ambiguity about the experiences of loss and pain suffered; rather, it is an ambiguity about how we respond to such suffering. Our own reactions are questioned, because, after all, what is it in us that makes us seek out the stories of another's grief? Or, even more problematically, what makes us follow the stories of the torturers? We follow Ubu's history, are drawn into his family drama, are confronted with his logics of self-justification. We as audience are also implicated because we laugh at his sometimes absurd antics, and this very laughter accuses us.

This raises the question of dramatic structure. *Ubu and the Truth Commission*, as the title suggests, has Ubu as its central protagonist, and it sets the Commission against this individual. Our agent is thus, in a sense, an agent of evil. Why have we made this choice? Much of world literature has done the same. Even Milton, in *Paradise Lost*, finds himself as 'of the devil's party', so to speak. Narrative depend upon agency; the stories of those who 'do' are generally more compelling than those who are 'done to'. This is then one reason for our choice. Another has been determined by the nature of the Commission itself, which has cast those who are victims as the central protagonists of the human rights hearings. The stories we hear are, over and over, those of apparent bystanders who assert their unwarranted suffering. This is at one level appropriate, but as a result we tend not to hear about people who could be characterised as 'knowing participants' in a political war. The stories which we hear do not emphasize the accounts of those opponents of apartheid who were resourceful, energetic, resilient political activists. People are recast within the logics of mourning, and become inexplicable casualties of meaningless violence.

There is no doubt another reason why the Ubu-like perpetrator became our protagonist: he provoked us. He is familiar but wholly foreign, he is both human and inhuman. He is the limit term which was used to keep an entire system of meaning in place, from its most extreme to its most banal.

Thus while the TRC has had the two-fold purpose of documenting the cases of victims and of hearing the amnesty applications of perpetrators, it effectively has also been instrumental in creating a context for interrogating how and why such human rights abuses could occur. Ubu's story is, at one level, a singular story of individual pathology; yet it is at the same time an exemplary account of the relationships between capitalist ideology, imperialism, race, class, and gender, religion and modernisation in the southern African sub-region.

The Writing Process

The first phase was a discussion with William Kentridge, Basil Jones and Adrian Kohler, in which we agreed in principle about using Ubu to explore the TRC. At the end of 1996 we then had a series of workshops with the Handspring Puppet Company performers, during which period I got some sense of the actor's capacities, and was introduced to the basic style of performance of the puppets. During these workshops we also discussed some of the non-naturalistic elements which might be introduced, such as the three-headed dog. We engaged in a very free process of experimenting with new hybrid forms, somewhere between animation and puppetry, in which drawn figures were manipulated by hand, and then filmed frame by frame as a sequence of individual drawings, rather like the technique used for more conventional animation. Through these various workshops, those involved in the processes developed an increasing sense of the possibilities of the forms we were evolving. My writing emerged very much out of these explorations. One of the great advantages of working with

Handspring Puppet Company has been its own experiments in non-naturalistic idioms, which allowed us creative freedom, notwithstanding the weighty documentary imperatives of the TRC itself.

Through the workshops we determined that Pa and Ma Ubu would be played by live actors with no puppet equivalents. These characters thus exist, as it were, on one scale. The witnesses, who are represented by puppet-figures, exist on another scale, and a great deal of their meaning arises out of this fact. Puppets can provide an extraordinary dimension to a theatrical project of this kind, because every gesture, is as it were, metaphorized. The puppet draws attention to its own artifice, and we as audience willingly submit ourselves to the ambiguous processes that at once deny and assert the reality of what we watch. Puppets also declare that they are being 'spoken through'. They thus very poignantly and compellingly capture complex relations of testimony, translation and documentation apparent in the processes of the Commission itself.

Other puppet figures in the play allude in part to elements from Jarry. In *Ubu Cocu*, the sequel to *Ubu Roi*, for example, he has three diabolical agents, the Palcontents, who serve Ubu's manic acts of mayhem. These characters are invoked through the three-headed dog that in *Ubu and the Truth Commission* acts as an instrument of death and destruction.

Many of the writing choices which I have made have been contingent upon other factors, such as the particular animation styles used by William Kentridge, as well as the sophisticated puppeteering technologies of the Handspring Puppet Company. Further, this theatre company brings a performance style of great expressive care to the characters, an element which has determined what kinds of testimony have been appropriate for inclusion.

◆

Of the nineteen Truth Commissions held internationally, South Africa's is apparently the first to have public hearings. In this sense, our case is exceptional. However, in other terms *Ubu and the Truth Commission* does not explore a uniquely South African story. We in the late twentieth century live in an era of singular attention to questions of war crimes, reparations, global 'peace-keeping'. We are, it seems, increasingly aware of the obligation to hear testimony, even while we may yet be determining how to act upon what we have heard.

DIRECTOR'S NOTE

William Kentridge

The crocodile's mouth

In South Africa at the moment there is a battle between the paper shredders and the photostat machines. For each police general who is shredding documents of his past there are officers under him who are photostating them to keep as insurance against future prosecutions. On stage I wanted to show a shredding machine. But a real machine, noisily and slowly going through reams of paper, did not seem very remarkable. We thought of using a bread slicer on stage as a metaphor, but were daunted by the thought of all that wasted, sliced bread each night. We thought of doing a drawing or animation of the shredding machine, and projecting it on screen, but I baulked at the thought of those hours of drawing the spaghetti trails of shredded paper. Then we thought. We already have three dogs on stage, why not feed the evidence we want to shred, to a dog? But their mouths were too small to swallow a video tape or ream of documents. So we asked, what has a wide enough mouth to swallow whatever we want to hide? Hence the crocodile's mouth.

The TRUTH AND RECONCILIATION COMMISSION is an enquiry established in terms of the negotiated settlement between the outgoing Nationalist government and the incoming ANC government of South Africa. The brief of the Commission is to examine human rights abuses that occurred in South Africa over the past thirty-five years. There are two parts to this process. Victims and survivors come to the Commission to recount their stories of what happened to them or members of their families (many of those involved did not survive their story and it is left to mothers and brothers to give evidence). The second part of the process is the amnesty hearings in which perpetrators of these abuses may give evidence of what they have done. Their inducement? A full confession can bring amnesty and immunity from prosecution or civil procedures for the crimes committed. Therein lies the central irony of the Commission. As people give more and more evidence of the things they have done they get closer and closer to amnesty and it gets more and more intolerable that these people should be given amnesty.

The Commission itself is theatre, or at any rate a kind of ur-theatre. Its hearings are open to the public, as well as being televised and broadcast on the radio. Many of the hearings are presided over by Archbishop Tutu in full purple magnificence. The hearings move from town to town setting up in a church hall, a school auditorium. In each setting the same set is erected. A table for the witnesses (always at least as high as that of the commissioners so the witnesses never have to look up to the commissioners.) Two or three glass booths for the translators. A large banner hangs on the wall behind the commissioners, <u>TRUTH THROUGH RECONCILIATION</u>. One by one witnesses come and have their half hour to tell their story, pause, weep, be comforted by professional comforters who sit at the table with them. The stories are harrowing, spellbinding. The audience sit at the edge of their seats listening to every word. This is exemplary civic theatre, a public hearing of private griefs which are absorbed into the body politic as a part of a deeper understanding of how the society arrived at its present position. This theatre rekindles each day the questions of the moment. How to deal with a guilt for the past, a memory of it. It awakes every day the conflict between the desire for retribution and a need for some sort of social reconciliation. Even those people (and there are a lot) who will have nothing to do with the Commission and who are in denial of the truths it is revealing are, in their very strident refusals, joining in the debate.

Both the process of the Commission and material coming out of it have been a source of new theatre being made in South Africa. Three plays have run at the Market theatre complex in Johannesburg that deal with our recent past and the Commission.

But in the face of the strength of the theatre of the Commission, the question arises, how can any of us working in the theatre compete with it? Of course we can't and don't try to. The origin of our work is very different and even if in the end it links directly to the Commission, this is secondary rather than primary. Our theatre is a reflection on the debate rather than the debate itself. It tries to make sense of the memory rather than be the memory.

To go on a fast and brief digression into the origin of this our most recent play *Ubu and the Truth Commission*: I have for some years been working with the Handspring Puppet Company in Johannesburg making pieces of theatre that combine animation, puppets and actors—not out of some deep aesthetic principle or programme, but rather out of the fact that I make animation, and Handspring make puppet theatre and we wanted to see what would happen if we combined the two. Some readers may have seen *Woyzeck on the Highveld* that we performed in 1993. And *Faustus in Africa* which we performed two years ago. Faustus was a huge undertaking

reconciliation through truth?

and after it was done the Handspring Puppet Company and I decided to do a minimal production—two actors, maybe one fragment of animation. Something we could do and survive. *Waiting for Godot* threw itself up as an option. It would work very well for puppets and perhaps only one fragment of animation in the middle when Lucky and Pozzo THINK. But we reckoned without the Beckett fundamentalists who would not give permission for us to leave out even a comma from the stage directions. We then thought how we could find a neo-Becketian text to work with. None of us had the courage or skill to write our own text. We then thought of working with a Found Text: this in the hope of finding in the words that people use to describe extreme situations, a bed rock connection between human experience and the language we use to talk about it. We thought of starting on a project that would gather oral testimonies from land-mine victims waiting in rural orthopaedic hospitals in Angola and Mozambique. This project was called *Waiting Room*.

At about this time I was working on a series of etchings based on Jarry's Ubu (for an exhibition marking the centenary of the first production of *Ubu Roi* on stage in Paris. These etchings involved a drawing of a naked man in front of a blackboard. On the blackboard were chalk drawings of Jarry's Ubu with his pointed head and belly spiral. After the etchings were done I wanted to animate the chalk Jarryesque drawings: and then thought that if the chalk drawings were animated, so should the figure in front be. I then asked a choreographer friend if she wanted to do a dance piece using a dancer in front of a screen in which a schematic line drawing of Ubu would be moving. Thus the Ubu project was begun. Panic mounted. I realised I could not do both the *Ubu* and *Waiting Room* projects. There were not enough weeks for animation. In desperation I combined the two.

At this time too the first hearings of the Truth Commission began and it rapidly became clear that if we were looking for found texts we had an avalanche of remarkable material arriving every day. Even as I started the process of convincing the participants in the different projects that it made sense to combine them, it became clear that in some ways the contradictory projects—sober documentary material and wild burlesque—could make sense together. The material from the Truth Commission could give a *gravitas* and grounding to *Ubu* (which always had a danger of becoming merely amusing). At the same time the wildness and openness of Jarry's conception could give us a way of approaching the documentary material in a new way and so enable us all to hear the evidence afresh.

This was the central challenge we started with. Only now, with the production completed and on the stage, can we get any feeling whether the inauthenticity of the origins of the piece has damned it ineluctably or whether in spite of (or as I believe) because of, this strange, only half-coherent beginning, were we able to find pieces of the play, images, literary conceits, changing physical metaphors that we would never have arrived at if we had started from a sober beginning. How can we do honour to this material from the Truth Commission? In so far as I have a polemic it is this: to trust in the inauthentic, the contingent, the practical as a way of arriving at meaning. I will elaborate on this later.

A question that arose was how to deal with the witness's stories on the stage—these formed the Found Text of the original project. Quite early on we knew that the witnesses would all be performed by puppets (with the speaking manipulators visible next to them—our usual way of working) and that Ma and Pa Ubu would be played by actors.

There were two routes to this decision. The first as an answer to the ethical question: what is our responsibility to the people whose stories we are using as raw fodder for the play? There seemed to be an awkwardness in getting an actor to play the witnesses—the audience being caught halfway between having to believe in the actor for the sake of the story, and also not believe in the actor for the sake of the actual witness who existed out there but was not the actor. Using a puppet made this contradiction palpable. There is no attempt to make the audience think the wooden puppet or its manipulator is the actual witness. The puppet becomes a medium through which the testimony can be heard.

But it would be false to say that our route to the decision to use puppets for these parts came this way. Rather we knew from the beginning that Pa and Ma Ubu would be human actors as that had been the premise for the first dance/animation conception, and by the same token, we knew that the witnesses would be puppets because that had been the premise of the *Waiting Room* project. The more honourable route to the decision about performance style, the first 'ethical' route, is a justification after the event.

But the decision brought a whole series of meanings and opportunities in its wake, the most important of which was that witnesses could appear in different corners of Ubu's life, not only at the witness stand as we had originally anticipated. They were also able to generate a whole series of unexpected meanings that became central to the play. For example, we experimented with a scene in which Ubu is lying on a table and above him a puppet witness gives evidence on the death of his child. We tried it first with the witness standing behind Ubu's hips. The body of Ubu became an undulating landscape, a small rise in the ground behind which the witness spoke. We then tried the same scene with the witness behind Ubu's head. Immediately the testimony of the witness became a mere dream of Ubu, the story was taken from the witness and became Ubu's confession. We put the witness behind Ubu's legs again and he was back in the landscape. We then tried to see how close the puppet could get to touching Ubu without breaking the double image. Extremely close we found. And then we tried it with the witness touching Ubu's hip with its wooden hand. An extraordinary thing happened. What we saw was an act of absolution. The witness forgave, even comforted Ubu for his act. These were a series of wholly unexpected meanings, generated not through clarity of thought , or brilliance of invention, but through practical theatre work. This is the second polemic I would make. A faith in a practical epistemology in the theatre—trusting in and using the artifices and techniques of theatre to generate meaning.

It also works in reverse. With the animation dance scene, I had the clear idea of creating a character made up of the live actor in front of the screen and a schematic representation or cartoon of the same character on the screen. Both would be seen together and together would generate the richly complex person. Confidence in this idea gave the strength to begin the project. However, it became clear within twenty minutes of starting this that it would not work. For reasons of synchronisation, parallax, lighting, stilted performance, it became impossible and this central principle was thrown out. Next polemic—Mistrust of Good Ideas in the abstract. Mistrust of starting with a knowledge of the meaning of an image and thinking it can then be executed. There is for me more than an accidental linguistic connection between *executing* an idea and *killing* it.

But to go back to the question of the witnesses and their testimonies which is the central question we grappled with in the heart of our play. As I have said our solution was to use puppets. (Even here it was not quite so simple. At first we realised how brilliant was our conception of using puppets because, at the Commission, not only did one have witnesses giving evidence, but one also had a translator of that evidence. Two speakers for the same story and *our puppets need two manipulator*s. One manipulator could tell the story in Zulu and the other could translate. But it did not work. The stories could not be heard. In the end we banished our translators to a glass booth—Ubu's shower—and made a difference between the natural voice of the witness and the artificial public address voice of the translator.)

But there have been other solutions to the question of how to deal with the raw material thrown up by the Truth Commission. As I said earlier, there were two other plays running at the Market theatre that deal with the Truth Commission. The first, *The Dead Wait,* is a conventional play. It is a fictional reconstruction of an event from the war in Angola, recounting a soldier's return to South Africa and his attempt to make his confession for a crime he committed. Although this play comes out of the context of the Truth Commission, it is not directly about the Commission and its processes.

The other play, *The Story I Am About To Tell,* was made by a support group for survivors who have given evidence before the Commission. It is a play designed to travel around various communities to spread awareness of the Commission and engage people in debate around questions raised by the Commission. Their solution of how to deal with the testimonies of witnesses at the Commission was to have three of the witnesses play themselves. That is, three people who were giving evidence before the Truth and Reconciliation Commission returned each night, and on stage, give their evidence again. The mother of a lawyer whose head was blown up by a booby trapped walkman describes crawling on her knees into the room where the shattered body and head lay. A man describes three years on death row waiting to be hanged for a crime he did not commit. A woman describes being arrested, interrogated and raped by security police. Their evidence is the central, but not the only element of the play, most of which is set in a taxi full of people going to a Truth Commission hearing. Three professional actors play the bit parts, provide comic interludes, and lead the scripted debates about the Commission and the three 'real' people give their testimony.

And yet it is only a partial solution to the questions raised by the Commission. Because what the 'real' people give is not the evidence itself, but performances of the evidence. There is a huge gap between the testimony at the Commission and its reperformance on stage. And these are not actors. In fact it is their very awkwardness that makes their performances work. One is constantly thrown back, through their awkwardness, into realising these are the actual people who underwent the terrible things they are describing. The most moving moment for me was when one of the survivors (survivor of three years on death row) had a lapse of memory. How could he forget his own story—but of course he was in that moment a performer at a loss for his place in the script. I have no clear solution to the paradoxes this half testimony, half performance raised. But describe it as one of many possible ways of dealing with the material.

The Truth and Reconciliation Commission was faced with a similar problem of doing justice to the testimonies. There was a divergence between the emotions expressed by the witnesses telling their stories and the version given by the translators. It was felt that so much of the heart of the testimony was lost when it came back through the translators. So for a short while the Commission had the disastrous idea of encouraging the translators to copy the emotions of the witnesses and to perform the emotions in their translations. This was soon stopped.

The question of how to do justice to the stories bedevils all of us trying to work in this terrain. With *Ubu and the Truth Commission* the task is to get a balance between the burlesque of Pa and Ma Ubu and the quietness of the witnesses. When the play is working at its best, Pa Ubu does not hold back. He tries to colonise the stage and be the sole focus of the audience. And it is the task of the actors and manipulators of the puppets to wrest that attention back. This battle is extremely delicate. If pushed too hard there is the danger of the witnesses becoming strident, pathetic, self pitying. If they retreat too far they are swamped by Ubu. But sometimes, in a good performance, and with a willing audience we do make the witnesses stories clearly heard and also throw them into a wider set of questions that Ubu engenders around them.

It sounds recondite but again I will say that it is only on the stage, in the moment, that one can judge how the material is given its weight. This changes both from performance to performance and from audience to audience.

Purely in the context of my own work I would repeat my trust in the contingent, the inauthentic, the whim, the practical, as strategies for finding meaning. I would repeat my mistrust in the worth of Good Ideas. And state a belief that somewhere between relying on pure chance on the one hand, and the execution of a programme on the other, lies the most uncertain, but the most fertile ground for the work we do.

But I have no fixed opinion on which of the three plays I have referred to is the best way to go. I think I have shown that it is not the clear light or reason or even aesthetic sensibility which determines how one works, but a constellation of factors only some of which we can change at will.

Each of the different pieces of theatre I have described can and has had enormous impact on their respective audiences. After one performance of

The Story I Am About To Tell, a spectator was inconsolable. Her tears were for the stories, but also she said that they were for anger and regret, that never in her life in Munich had there been a similar theatre of testimony. A friend was deeply moved by the *Dead Wait,* the play about the war in Angola. He had served as a soldier in that war. And after a performance of *Ubu and the Truth Commission* a woman came up to us, obviously moved by what she had seen. She said she was from Romania. We expressed surprise that the play had been accessible to her as it was so local in its content. 'That's it,' she said. 'It is so local. So local. This play is written about Romania.'

PUPPETEERS' NOTE

Basil Jones and Adrian Kohler

The puppets were developed in response to the project's needs. Now, reviewing what was a fairly organic process, we can see that three types of puppet were used. Each has a particular relationship to Ma and Pa Ubu, the only two human characters in the play. So firstly, we have the vulture, secondly the dog and crocodile, and thirdly the witness puppets.

The vulture acts as a single chorus, providing sardonic commentary throughout the action of the play. It has a limited range of actions and a set of electronic squawks interpreted on the screen as proverbs. Thus it is a form of manipulation: like gears driven by motors which in turn are driven by a remote technician—which is appropriate to its function in the play—an apparently authorless automaton spewing forth programmed truisms.

Higher up the evolutionary scale are Brutus, the three-headed dog (with three visible manipulators) and Niles, the crocodile (with one visible manipulator). They move about in the same space as Pa and Ma Ubu and are not restricted to traditional puppet playboards such as were used in *Woyzeck on the Highveld*. The crocodile is Ma Ubu's handbag, but also Pa Ubu's pet advisor and cover-up man, using his big mouth as the shredder of Ubu's evidence.

The dog Brutus, is Ubu's henchman. When he goes out to do his evil work, it is the dog who does it with him. Their culpability is indivisible. As such, the dog's three characters, foot soldier, general and politician, share a single body made out of an old briefcase given by Braam Fischer to Sydney Kentridge.

Both of these characters are essentially puppets and it would be difficult to imagine how their roles could be played by human actors. For example, the crocodile has a mouth that can swallow fairly large objects and its belly is a large canvas bag (once the kit bag of Basil Jones' father when on military service in North Africa) for storing them. Here they are easily accessible for discovery by Ma Ubu. The single body of the dogs is a suitcase: an ideal place for Pa Ubu to plant incriminating evidence when the time comes for him to distance himself from their actions.

The final category of puppet is the witnesses. Their responsibility in the play is both central and extremely onerous, as their task is to re-enact the deeply harrowing personal accounts of the effect of the former Apartheid State on people's lives. Badly handled, such stories could easily become a kind of horror pornography. The puppets assist in mediating this horror. They are not actors playing a role. Rather, they are wooden dolls attempting to be real people. As they attempt to move and breathe as we do, they cross the barrier of the here and now and become metaphors for humanity. In this case, two puppeteers manipulate one puppet. The manipulators, working in concert, split and somehow reduce their individual responsibility for the puppet's actions and the puppet's speech. This encourages us to enter into the illusion that the puppet has a life and responsibility of its own. But the fact that the manipulators are present also allows us to use the emotions visible in the puppeteers' faces to inform our understanding of the emotions of the puppet character, with its immobile features.

The two presences supporting the puppet on either side give it a degree of symbolic vulnerability, and at the same time recall the people who comfort witnesses during TRC hearings. Puppets are brought to life by the conviction of the puppeteer and the willingness of the audience. When an actor plays opposite a puppet, she or he participates in the same process. There can be no eye contact with the puppeteer. The actor's focus is solely on the puppet itself. Puppet movement, particularly that of the witnesses, needs to find its correct speed. This is generally slower than the human equivalent to allow the audience to observe clearly what the figure is trying to do, whether it is an arm gesture, the turning of a head, or the picking up or placing of an object by the figure. Working with a particular figure will enable the puppeteer to determine its puppet speed. Moments of physical touching between actor and puppet are carefully worked out. The difference between the materials of which a puppet is made and human flesh can break the illusion that both exist in the same moment.

The main parts of the puppets are made of wood. The rough carving ensures that the puppets' faces have a surface well-keyed for illumination. Therefore, under the lights, the movement of tiny shadows cast by the gouging chisel, particularly the contrast between looking up, looking forward and looking down, assists the illusion of changing expressions on an otherwise immobile face.

These wooden dolls attempting to be people are never seen by Ma and Pa Ubu, though their actions impact fundamentally on their lives. Though they occupy the same space, using the same furniture behind which to perform, they appear to be somewhere else. The Ubus eat the goods they loot from the Spaza shop, but cannot see the shopkeeper, who in turn cannot see them. This division between the human clowns and the puppets, mirrors the era of trauma the play describes.

The text for *Ubu and the Truth Commission* was commissioned by William Kentridge and Handspring Puppet Company. The play was first showcased at The Laboratory, the Market Theatre, Johannesburg on 26 May 1997. The world premier took place on 17 June 1997 at the Kunsfest, Weimar, with the following cast:

CAST

Pa Ubu:	Dawid Minaar
Ma Ubu:	Busi Zokufa
Puppet Characters:	Basil Jones, Adrian Kohler, Louis Seboko, Busi Zokufa
Director:	William Kentridge
Stage Manager and Video Operator:	Bruce Koch
Sound Technician:	Simon Mahoney
Company and Tour Manager:	Wesley France

PRODUCTION CREDITS

Animation:	William Kentridge
Assistant Animators:	Tau Qwelane and Suzie Gabie
Choreography:	Robyn Orlin
Puppet Master:	Adrian Kohler
Assistant Puppet Maker:	Tau Qwelane
Music:	Warrick Sony and Brendan Jury
TRC Research:	Antjie Krog
Lighting Design:	Wesley France
Sound Design:	Wilbert Schübel
Film Editor:	Catherine Meyburgh
Film and Video Research:	Gail Behrmann
Costumes:	Adrian Kohler and Sue Steele
Set Design:	William Kentridge and Adrian Kohler
Production Co-ordinator:	Basil Jones

Special thanks are due to the following institutions whose financial assistance made this production possible: Art Bureau, München; Kunstfest Weimar; Migros Kulturprozent, Switzerland; Niederersächsisches Staatstheater, Hannover (Schauspiel); The Standard Bank Arts Festival; The Department of Arts, Culture, Science and Technology; The Market Theatre Foundation.

Produced by Mannie Manim Productions, Johannesburg and Thomas Petz, Art Bureau, München. The play is protected by copyright. All requests for performance rights should be addressed to Mannie Manim Productions, P O Box 18, Wits 2050, South Africa.
Fax 011 339 1502, e-mail: manimpro@ iafrica.com

UBU AND THE TRUTH COMMISSION

ACT ONE: 1

When the scene opens, there is a puppet near centre stage, making soup. Music in the background is tender, quiet. For several minutes the soup-making is undertaken, from cutting of vegetables, to stirring, to salting. The soup is tasted twice in this process. On the second tasting, the scene changes abruptly.

ACT ONE: 2

The shift in scene is inaugurated by a change in music. The earlier piece is abruptly replaced by a brash, harsh, cartoonish piece. We find ourselves in the Ubu home. There is a vulture-puppet on a stick (which stays on stage for much of the action, as it is the source of the axioms which will emerge on the projection screen throughout). There is also a small column upon which a witness-puppet is making a pot of soup. As Pa Ubu strides on stage, he kicks over the soup-maker, with no evident sense of what it is that he has done. The puppet drops, and is carried off by one of the two puppeteers. The other puppeteer is transformed into Ma Ubu, who proceeds with the scene. Pa Ubu strikes a pose, holding his injured foot, as if he has stubbed it on a stone.

PA UBU: Pschitt!!

MA UBU: Oooh! What a nasty word. Pa Ubu, you're a dirty old man.

Ma Ubu and Pa Ubu begin a dance-like chase: they alternately pursue each other, snarling with rage, then are triggered into dance poses and smiling freezes. After several such moments, Ma Ubu and Pa Ubu flounce away from each other, begin a fight-dance.

ACT ONE: 3

At the back of the stage is a large projection screen. Images of various kinds are projected onto this surface, and the performers at times interact with and at times seem

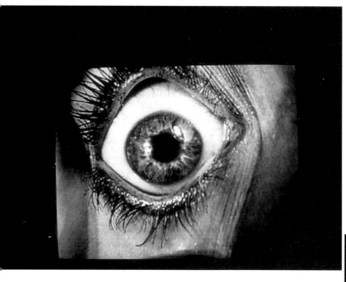

It has not been possible to repro-
duce the full effect of the animated
sequences which are projected
onto the screen behind the actors
during performances. For that matter, being projected images, they do
not photograph well either.
Nonetheless, several fragments
from these sequences are repro-
duced here and in the 'flip-file' on
the opposite pages.

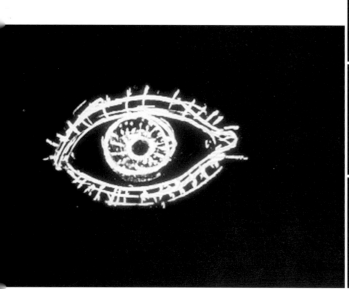

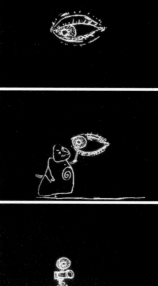

*oblivious of the visual field which is behind them. In the opening
sequence, several of the major motifs are introduced: the Ubu mannekin,
the camera tripod, and the all-seeing eye.*

The first credits appear on the projection screen.

ACT ONE: 4

PA UBU: *(Holding his foot, which has been hurt by the kick.)* And
bugger, and damn! Our favourite foot has taken a mortal blow,
because our wife cannot keep the house clean. I am dying!

MA UBU: Your trotters can't kill you, unless that's where you keep your
brains!

PA UBU: Madam, we do not spend all day taking care of the affairs of
state, to be insulted in our own castle!

MA UBU: You shouldn't worry about the affairs of state, but the state of
your affairs!

PA UBU: And what, you old cow, do you mean by that?

MA UBU: Just this—if you spend another night with your bitches, you
can sleep in the shed with your dogs!

PA UBU: We are offended by your accusations, Mother.

MA UBU: And I am offended by your nocturnal activities, which have
addled your brain, so that you see no further than your nose.

PA UBU: By my green candle …

MA UBU: Which is a miserable little organ, as I know.

PA UBU: Ma, you go too far. I will bash your head in and never say sorry.

MA UBU: I go too far? Let's go one step further. Where were you last
night?

PA UBU: Madam, we were busy with our business. The precise nature of
our—undertaking—is classified.

MA UBU: Pooh, as to that! The signs of your lust have given you away.
I've seen the red on your collar, and tufts of hair on your sleeve.

The vulture is the only mechanically operated puppet in the production. It functions as a detached commentator, rather like a chorus, and is thus never associated with a puppeteer.

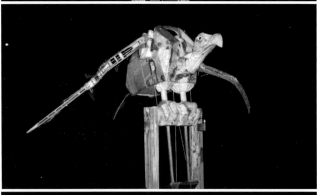

PA UBU: It is regrettable that our wife has chosen to fix her attentions on the domestic laundry when she would have found a more appropriate activity in tidying our house, so that at our day's end our corpulent self could enter at ease, instead of stumbling over the furniture. We demand that you take more care over securing a safe passage for our nimble self.

MA UBU: Pfarrt and Pshitt! Keep your secrets, then. But if you come back to me with the smell of your women upon you, I'll find you out, do you hear me! And when I find you out, I'll cut you out and throw you out.

PA UBU: Damn you, Madam. We will not be accused by you!

MA UBU: Who has more right to accuse than I?

PA UBU: Question dismissed! Next!

MA UBU: Who do you see each night?

PA UBU: Question dismissed! Next!

MA UBU: Who owns your heart?

Lights out. Ma Ubu exits. Lights up. Pa Ubu is standing alone.

PA UBU: *To himself, facing the audience, smelling into the palm of his hands, a look of horror and disgust. Pause. Collects himself. Pa Ubu sweeps up the vegetables which were scattered across the stage by his kick.*

My good lady wife would not complain if she understood the work that takes me out at night. Once I was an agent of the state, and had agency and stature. The country's money was in my safe-keeping, as I had blown up the safe and its keeper. I administered the funds to myself, to save the nation the burden of doing so. Now, after my years of loyal service, I find myself cast aside without thanks. My enemies are everywhere, and we therefore have to cover our back while at the same time protecting our strumpot, so that we are always defended.

The vulture puppet on a stick squawks, and the first vulture text appears on the screen: **After the third fire on the roof, keep a bucket on the stairs.**

ACT ONE: 5

A table is wheeled on stage, with Brutus, the three-headed dog. The dog enters, sniffs the air, begins howling. Pa Ubu enters.

PA UBU: Shut up, you pack of lies, or I'll split you end to end and feed you to Ma's kitty. Holy sherbert! How is a man to maintain his dignity if he cannot even control his dogs?

The dogs rub affectionately against Pa Ubu.

HEAD ONE: *(panting with excitement)* So, boss, where to tonight, boss? What's in it for us? Some little bone, eh? A tiny cartilaginous morsel, still fragrant and warm?

HEAD TWO: As for me, I'm of another breed: I don't want to bite, but I do long to lead.

HEAD THREE: While these brutes can carry out raids for the nation, diplomacy needs more informed conversation. What secret, special and covert activities are to be executed tonight? We only need to know, so that we know what to deny.

PA UBU: We will tell you what you need to know. Remember, we are the tail that wags the dog.

DOGS, TOGETHER: Right, captain. You're the boss. We're your creature.

At this point Pa Ubu and the dogs sing a scat quartet together.

PA UBU: Not any old dog is a man's best friend
Who'd service and obey as I intend.
To get what I need
I selectively breed
'Til his parts make the whole in a singular blend.

With razor-like teeth and with steel-sprung jaw
I've found myself a weapon that evades the law.
He'll attack when he's told
And submit when I scold
For I've now made a pet of the dogs-of-war.

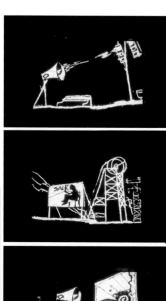

The Evening ST ROLL.

DOGS: Not any old dog is a man's best friend
       Who'd service and obey as he'd intend.
       To get what he needs
       He selectively breeds
       'Til our parts make the whole in a singular blend.

       With razor-like teeth and with steel-sprung jaw
       We now provide a weapon that evades the law.
       We'll attack when we're told
       And submit should he scold
       For we're old Pa Ubu's dogs-of-war.

PA UBU: Okay, enough of that. Come on boys.

Pa Ubu whistles for the dogs as he exits. The whistle should be distinctive, a four or five note whistle. This whistle will recur throughout the play, at points at which the audience should be reminded of the dogs' activities in the world. The whistle will thus serve as a kind of 'leitmotif', signalling a collaboration between Pa Ubu and his dogs. On the screen, we see images suggesting the dogs' evening walk. As they stop looking for direction, he speaks into an imaginary radio transmitter in his underpants.

PA UBU: Hello? Ja Generaal. Ja, Generaal. Nee, seker nie. Alles is in order.
          Presies, ja. Ja Generaal. Over and out.

They continue until they reach their destination at which point we hear an explosion.

ACT ONE: 6

*Back home in the Ubu household. Ma Ubu is brought on stage, in her armchair. On screen is the caption **Ma Ubu Dreams of Love and Money**. She engages in a solo tap dance full of fantasies of unattained riches and adoration.*

Ma Ubu collapses exhausted onto her armchair. A moment or two of silence. Then offstage sounds of barking; noises off as Pa Ubu returns home: key in lock, etc.

Pa Ubu switches on a light. He is to one side of the stage, in the glass booth which is used as a shower. Ma Ubu lies in her armchair. A soft spotlight comes on, to show Pa Ubu in the shower.

The **SMELL** ↙
of BLOOD and **DYNAMITE**

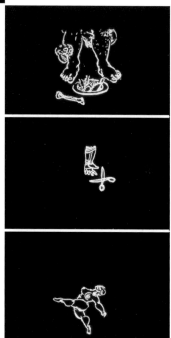

MA UBU: Is that you, Pa? PAAA? *(Her voice in the background while Pa Ubu showers.)* Washing, washing, washing. Every night it's the same. You come back home, used up and tired. And I must say nothing. What is it, Pa Ubu, that you wash away?

CAPTION ON SCREEN: ***The Smell of Blood and Dynamite.***

MA UBU: It's sex, isn't it? It's sex.

Drawings of Pa Ubu's fantasies appear on the screen. Pa Ubu sings "Hier's ek weer". As he emerges from the shower, Ma Ubu pursues him.

MA UBU: Just because I've stood it till now doesn't mean I will take it for ever, you know! I'm telling you, I'll make you pay!

ACT TWO: 1

VOICE OVER MICROPHONE: Sound of someone tapping a live microphone. Overhead, a voice speaks:

VOICE OF TRC: Can you hear my voice clearly? Good. Can you hear the translator?

Puppeteer enters with witness puppet and microphone. To the left, Ma Ubu as translator in the booth, also with microphone.

CAPTION ON SCREEN: ***A Bath.*** *This quickly morphs to* ***A Bloodbath.***

WITNESS: **Queenstown yajika yaba yindawo yemfazwe.**
Queenstown became a battleground.

Amapolisa ayenyuka esehla ezintratweni bedubula wonke umntu.
The police drove up and down the streets, shooting at anyone and everyone.

Wathi akungabuyi unyana wam, kwathwa mandiyokumbuza kwi mortuary polisa.
When my son didn't come home, they said I should ask at the police mortuary.

Kulapho kwafuneka ndifanise isidumbu sonyanam.
It was there that I had to identify my son.

Pa Ubu's shower cubicle is also the
translation booth used during the
translation of witness's testimony.

Zazininzi izidumbu, zibaxakile.
There were so many bodies, they couldn't cope.

Salinda phambi kwe mortuary, uthotho lwegazi lwalubaleka lusuka phantsi komnyango, luvale idrain engaphandle.
We waited in front of the mortuary—a thick stream of blood was running from under the door—blocking the outside drain.

Ngaphakathi, ivumba lalilibi.
Inside, the smell was terrible.

Izidumbu zipakene esinye phezu kwesinye.
Bodies were stacked upon each other.

Igazi lalise lijike laba luhlaza.
The blood was already turning green.

Ndazixelela ukuba, noba bangabe benzentoni emntaneni wam, ndizakumbona ngophawu esilvini.
I said to myself, no matter what they have done to my child, I can identify him because of the mark on his chin.

Ndaya e mortuary.
I went to the morgue.

Ndambona apho umntwanam.
There I saw my child.

Ndalubona uphawu esilevini.
I saw the mark on his chin.

Kodwa ndathi kubo, hayi, asingomntwana wam lo.
But I said to them, this is not my child.

Asingomntwana wam lo.
This is not my child.

Asingomntwana wam lo.
This is not my child.

ACT TWO: 2

Dim lighting. Pa Ubu is wheeled in behind the table. He is drinking. On screen, animation of a radio which keeps on transmogrifying into a cat. The cat-radio taunts

The *LIGHT*
of TRUTH

Pa Ubu. Pa Ubu cowers under a large chair. His backside projects out from under the chair. Ma Ubu enters, carrying her handbag, which is also a puppet of a crocodile.

MA UBU: What's going on here, in the dark?

She switches on the lights.

CAPTION ON SCREEN: ***The Light of Truth***.

She places the bag down on the table, places Pa Ubu's bottle and glass in the bag. Ma Ubu notices Pa Ubu under the chair.

MA UBU: Pa, I see your rump under the chair. Get out here at once, or I'll brand your beef.

PA UBU: Go away, whoever you are. There's no-one here but us rats.

MA UBU: *(To audience)* It may be a rat, but it has only two legs! *(To Ubu)* Very well, then, but first let me catch my breath.

Sits on chair above Pa Ubu.

PA UBU: Shittabugger, what a stench down here. A man could die of it. MA! Get up or you'll murder your husband.

MA UBU: Could it be—my gracious lord and noble master—his arse like a turnip half underground?

PA UBU: We were checking to determine whether the rotation of the earth's axis had produced an incline of the perpendicular to the horizontal. For the scrutiny of which, we had to prostrate ourselves, as you see.

MA UBU: Did you say, castrate yourself, you great booby? What is this feeble display of cowardice? Did I give up my life for this? Get up, you fool.

PA UBU: *(Clambering out, blubbering with fear)* SSSHHHH! Not a word. Don't tell them I'm here. O my poor head. I'll lose my ears. I used to be fearless, but soon I'll be earless!

MA UBU: It's not your ears I'll cut off! Don't flatter yourself, Pa. If some woman's husband is coming to get you, he can have you.

Ma Ubu storms out in a fury. Pa Ubu falls on his knees, and prays.

PA UBU: O the blood, O the blood,
  O the blood of the lamb sets me free,
  Send a flood, send a flood,
  Send your blood like a flood over me.

While Pa Ubu is on his knees, Niles, the crocodile puppet, comes to life.

NILES: Ah, Captain, you seem to be in something of a lather.
  What's up? Another fight with Ma?

PA UBU: Oh, Niles, such a vision I had. I saw the Great Truth approaching, a rope in its hand. It demanded I speak of the truth of our land.

NILES: Well, as I understand things, you have a choice. You can take your
  chances, keep silent, and wait to see if the law comes after you. But
  once they have unmasked you, you'll have to face the music. My
  advice would be to pre-empt it all. I hear there is to be a Commission
  to determine Truths, Distortions and Proportions.

PA UBU: I've heard of Truths, and know Distortions, but what are these
  Proportions you talk about?

NILES: An inquiry is to be conducted by great and blameless men who
  measure what is done, and why, and how.

PA UBU: And just what can these brilliant mathemunitions do?

NILES: They can beyond all ambiguity indicate when a vile act had a
  political purpose.

PA UBU: And if they so resolve?

NILES: Then they can and must absolve. The righteous have to forgive the
  unrighteous. It's the way of the world. But a full disclosure is what
  they demand. If they should find any dirt under your finger-nails after
  you have had a complete manicure, they will chop off your hands.

PA UBU: So—a full confession?

NILES: Quite.

PA UBU: Place my own neck in the noose? It is a poor tailor who has to
  make his own suits. Besides, our Reign of Terror was no Reign of Error.

We knew what we did, and still we did it.

NILES: All you did was your job. And really, what harm did you do? A little killing here and there never hurt anyone.

PA UBU: But if I keep mum, how will they find out? I still have friends in high places.

The vulture puppet on a stick squawks, and the following text appears on the screen: **More killers than saints have dined with princes.**

NILES: I'd advise you, speak before you are spoken to.

PA UBU: Never! A man is a man of honour, or a man is not a man.

NILES: A man is not a man when his necktie is made of rope.

PA UBU: WAAAAH! Save us!

NILES: Old Ubu, wait. Let us conduct an experiment after the pattern of the state. (*He picks up two of the oranges.*) These two orbs will measure the man. This, in your right hand, equals your honour, and in your left, it equals your fear. Now weigh your fear and honour in each hand: which has greater weight?

Together they mime this weighing.

PA UBU: It is most sinister. This, here, in my left hand, this fear of mine, it pulls the scale down. The massive and cumbrous burden of our millstone fright makes into airy nothing the counterpose of our valour. Niles, we have thus demonstrated by reason and scientific verification, that WE ARE A COWARD!

Partial blackout. Niles Exits, while Pa Ubu gasps with impotent fear. Ma Ubu enters.

ACT TWO: 3

MA UBU: Pa, you great baby! You sound as if you're afraid of your own shadow!

PA UBU: Wh—wh—who? wh—wh—what?

MA UBU: Father! Pull yourself together.

The CONSOLATIONS
of the FLESH

PA UBU: For—for—forgery—forgive me.

MA UBU: What is this? Do you truly repent? If you promise, no more women …

PA UBU: What? Oh, yes, yes. (Aside) Our foolish self almost betrayed us. (To Ma Ubu): Forgive me, Ma. I love only you!

CAPTION ON SCREEN: *The Consolations of the Flesh*.

A dance interlude. Ma Ubu comes down from the chair. Pa Ubu seizes her in his arms, and they dance 'langarm'. As they dance in front of the audience during this scene, they each address the audience, holding temporary friezes, while the music volume drops.

MA UBU: (To audience) A woman wants to be wanted. So we take them back. Always, we take them back, but nothing changes.

Dancing. Freeze. Music volume drops.

PA UBU: (To audience) I must, above all things, hide my stories from Ma. Who knows how she might react? Thus we must keep our own council. After all, to betray our men is to damn ourself. We can bravely face their exposure, but are a little more circumspect about our own. Therefore a soldier must bite his tongue. Furthermore, we are piously shocked by this confession nonsense. Gallons of blood and then gallons of tears to wash the walls clean.

Pa Ubu dances Ma Ubu off.

PA UBU: And Ma? She has no idea of what she says, for she has no idea of who I was. We would burn down the world before we would give away our country.

An animation sequence on screen (in which a pig's head is blown up by rigged earphones) links this to the next scene.

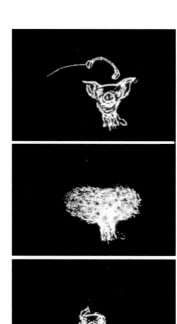

ACT TWO: 4

The second witness puppet enters, with puppeteer.

WITNESS: **Sebakanyana ga tsena mongwe mme a re, ba fisa ngwana wa gago.**
Someone came and told me, they are burning your son.

Ka simolola ka matha.
I started to run.

Ke ne ke sa itse kwa ke ne keya teng, ke ne ke matha fela.
I don't know where to, I just ran.

Ebe e le gore basadi bangwe ba mpiletsa morago.
Then some women called me back.

'Tlaya kwango, ba tsene jaana.'
'Come here, they went this way.'

Ga ke fitlha kwateng ba ne ba motsentse taere mo mmeleng, ba mo tshetse ka petrolo.
When I arrive there they have put a tyre around his body, they've doused him with petrol.

Ba mpha letlhokwana la metshisi le letukang gore ke le lathele kwa go ene.
And they then gave me a burning match to throw onto him.

Ka letlhela letlhokwana kwa morago ga legetla me.
I threw the match over my shoulder.

Ba mpha le lengwe gape mme ba ntse be ntshosa.
They gave me one again and threatened me.

Ka le lathela kwa morago ga legetla la me.
I threw it over my shoulder.

Ke dirile jalo go fitlhela bone ba lathela letlokwana le letukang mo mmeleng wa agwe.
I kept on doing that until they threw a burning match on his body.

A tshwara mollo.
He caught flame.

Ebe e legore ba tshaba.
Then they ran away.

This image of the trader-puppet setting up his streetside store, represents what is taking place in the centre of the Ubus' dining table, while Ma and Pa carry on with their meal at either end of the table. Visually, the photographs of Ma and Pa on pages 26 and 28 supplement this image, showing the separate but conflicting worlds of the Ubus and the witness puppets.

Go ne ga salla nna go lwela bophelo ba gagwe.
And it was left to me to fight for his life.

Ka matha go ya go batla metsi, ga seke ga thusa.
I ran to get water, but it didn't help.

Kelekile go mo gasa ka mmu.
I tried to put soil on him.

Mme o ne o semontsi.
But there wasn't enough.

Bofelong ka tima malakabe ka kobo.
Eventually I killed the flames with a blanket.

Ka motshwara.
I hold him.

Mmele othe wa gagwe one o tshele kwa ntle ga nko.
His whole body was burned except his nose.

O ne a nteba.
He looked up at me.

Molomo wa gagwe o bulega—o tswlega.
His mouth opened—and closed.

O bulegwa—o tswalega.
Opened—and closed.

Taaka wa nonyane.
Like a bird's.

Morago matlho a gagwe a fetola mmala.
Then his eyes changed—their colour.

Lights out.

An animation sequence links this to the following scene.

ACT TWO: 5

The stage is empty, except for the table. A puppet enters. The puppet takes centre-stage, setting up bits and pieces for his Spaza shop in the middle of the table. He has Jik, methylated spirits, as well as various oddments, bottles of lotion. In the

Throughout the play, the difference in scale and performance-style between the witness puppets and Ma and Pa Ubu is exploited. In this scene, the puppet's activities are focused and detailed, and he is silent in his ritual. Ma and Pa Ubu, by contrast, big and loud, assault one another during their dinner. The puppet is situated in the centre of the Ubu's dining table, but he is not aware of their presence, except through the effect they have upon him when they plunder his store for their meal.

background, the sound-track of someone selling street wares sets the mood. The process of setting up shop is slow and deliberate. While this proceeds, Ma Ubu and Pa Ubu settle down at the table to eat. They are unaware of the individual presence of the shop-keeper, but become aware of the goods on offer, which they take, gradually and cavalierly, as if all things are available for their own consumption. The shop-keeper throughout is unaware of who steals his belongings, although he is painfully aware of their disappearance. He has a limited arc of vision, so that he never looks at either extreme end of the table, where the Ubus sit.

Pa Ubu strides in.

PA UBU: FOOD, Madam, FOOOOOOD! Nothing like a bit of fear to fuel a man's appetite. We are so hungry we could eat a nag. What slop have you prepared?

MA UBU: *(Voice off)* Are your hands clean?

PA UBU: *(To audience)* By no means. My carrion acts cling to my digits like gloves. But the feeding of our appetites helps us to forget.

Pa Ubu sits down at one end of the table, hammering with his eating utensils.

PA UBU: *(Hammering on table)* MAA—If you keep me hungry, you make me angry. You don't want to see me angry, Mother.

MA UBU: *(Entering with bowls)* I don't want to see you at all, you ugly rhinoceros.

PA UBU: Hippopotamus!

MA UBU: Warthog!

PA UBU: Jellyfish!

MA UBU: Eel!

PA UBU: *(Tasting food)* Mmmmm, delicious seasoning, our mother.

MA UBU: I'm pleased you like it, our father.

Pause.

During the following dialogue, Ma Ubu and Pa Ubu help themselves to items from the Spaza shop.

PA UBU: *(Eating; muttering aloud)* First thing tomorrow, we'll remove the evidence and blow up his arse.

MA UBU: Well, at last! And then you can bury the bones.

PA UBU: *(Startled, looks up at Ma Ubu)* What?

MA UBU: I said, you can dig over that patch at the back and clear out the stones.

PA UBU: Aaaah, of course.

Ma Ubu and Pa Ubu begin to help themselves from the Spaza shop, and eat. Ma Ubu examines the price on one item.

MA UBU: I see that prices are still rising.

PA UBU: What uprising?

MA UBU: Today, everything costs an arm and a leg.

PA UBU: I had nothing to do with it!

MA UBU: Pass me the salt.

PA UBU: Who said it was assault?

MA UBU: Pa?

Pa Ubu looks up at Ma Ubu as if he doesn't recognize her. She however ignores him, takes some snuff, sneezes.

PA UBU: It looks like brain.

MA UBU: Mmmmm?

PA UBU: *(Looking absently ahead of him)* It looks like brain.

MA UBU: I spend hours, weeks, in the kitchen, and this is all you have to say? It's not fair, Pa! You don't appreciate me.

PA UBU: Psshii—shhh, shhh. Now, Ma, sorry, hey, sorry. Holy sherbert, this is good, really.

MA UBU: Thaaank you, Pa. *(She smiles warmly at him.)*

Pause. Pa Ubu reaches again for something from the Spaza shop. This time it is a box of poison.

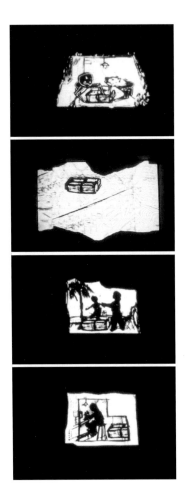

In this animation sequence we see Pa Ubu assisted by his dog making up a parcel. Pa Ubu flings the parcel on its way, and the package drifts over a series of map-like details. As we watch, the parcel settles over and over again; now in a house, now in a bar. Each time the parcel comes to rest, it blows up, transforming the original drawing into a blast-site.

PA UBU: *(Holding up poison)* By my shittabrush! We are beset on every side! Even our wife is trying to poison us. What is this mortal potion doing on our dining table? Let me assure you, madam, you could kill us as easily with your cooking!

MA UBU: Pooh, as to that! Who knows how poison finds its way? As they say, the knife finds its own sheath.

PA UBU: Silence, baggage! To turn against your husband is treason against the state. Therefore, Ma, we accuse you of treasonous acts, for which the penalty is beheading.

MA UBU: Judge not, Pa. And you know why.

PA UBU: NOT GUILTY! *(Pa Ubu collapses, defeated and dejected, after bellowing these words.)*

ACT TWO: 6

Lights out on stage. We hear Pa Ubu's whistle, over, which is followed by an animation sequence.

ACT TWO: 7

Puppeteer enters with witness puppet .

WITNESS: **Mapodisa a ne a tla go ntsaya mo ntlong yame.**
The police came to fetch me in my house.

Bare ba bone ditopo tsa bana rona, bare ke tsamaye le bone goya go dibona.
They said they had found the bodies of our children, they must take me to see them.

-—Ga ke dibona—
When I saw them—-

Di ne disena matlho.
They didn't have eyes.

Kajalo ka gopola gore mollo o phantse matlho a bone.
Well, I thought, the fire exploded their eyes out.

On the screen is a projection of a vast rotund shadow figure, after the classic figure of Jarry's conception. The actor performing the role of Pa Ubu emerges in front of the projection screen and responds to the sequence of shadow moves. The shadow finally makes whipping motions and Pa Ubu on stage reacts as if whipped.

Di ne disena golo fa ga tlhogo.
They didn't have this of the head *(indicating the top of the head with her hands, running the hands over the cranium)*.

E ne ele fela, ele fela golo fa—
It is just this, this, this part *(she rubs her forehead, above her brows)*.

Fa gone—gone goseyo.
This part *(indicating the top of the head)*. This part wasn't there.

Gape ba ne basena matsogo, ba sena maoto.
And they haven't got hands, they haven't got legs.

Puppet exits.

ACT TWO: 8

The scene begins with an animation sequence on the screen and the caption: **The Shadow-Dance**. *Finally, Pa Ubu rushes about the stage, retrieving things.*

NILES: Grrrrreetings, General. Here's a fine commotion. Do I smell the making of a covert operation?

PA UBU: Well, Niles, we took your advice under advisement, but have opted for concealing rather than revealing.

NILES: Not wise, old man. Some little breadcrumbs always lead the way back home.

PA UBU: Then you'll just have to help with cleaning up.

As he says this, Pa Ubu grabs Niles and begins to stuff documents down his throat. In the intervals, while Pa Ubu retrieves more pieces, Niles interjects.

NILES: What's this I taste?
A bit of skull shattered in pieces,
A pair of hands torn off at the wrists,
Some poisoned scalps shorn of their fleeces,
Some half-burned skin injected with cysts.

As they say, *fiat experimentum in corpore vili*, that is, let experiment be made on a worthless body. But here are some tougher bits, not so easily digested.

A piece of tongue that would not be silent,
A beaten back that ignored the ache,
A hand up-raised in gesture defiant,
A blood-red heart that would not break.
Here, Cap'n. These oddments you feed me are most
unsavoury. *(Burps)* Hello, that bit tasted familiar.

PA UBU: Eat up, Niles, there's a good boy, or you'll find yourself
attached to a pair of leather soles.

Stuffing Niles again.

NILES: OOOhh—I recognise that. It's given me quite a lump in my throat.

Pa Ubu stuffs Niles.

NILES: But, I say, I think you've left out one or two things. What about
those meaty bits in the bottom drawer?

PA UBU: Damn and blast! What do you know of these matters? *(He
dashes over to retrieve film reels, stuffs them into Niles.)*

NILES: MMMMMmmmm. *(Makes satisfied noises)* Delectable! Still, where's
the main course? How about that bag of tricks in your bedroom?

PA UBU: Shittabugger! *(He dashes off stage, brings back a bag of crumpled
bits and pieces, that he stuffs into Niles.)*

NILES: And the box in the bathroom cupboard?

PA UBU: Buggerashitt! Information is the beacon of our enlightenment,
but a man is cursed when his information is turned to shine on himself. *(He dashes off, to retrieve more, stuffs it into Niles.)*

NILES: Now it's given me heart-burn. ENOUGH!! Secure the rest 'til later.
It's safe enough for now. OOOooooooh. *(Moaning with discomfort, he lies
down on the floor. Comments, to the audience, as he lies down.)* A little
knowledge is a dangerous thing. It is also not wise to know too much.
We only make ourselves safe by knowing all.

The vulture puppet on a stick squawks, and the following text appears on the screen:
It is enough for the zebra to know about grass.

Niles settles himself to sleep on the table, to digest his meal.

Lights out.

ACT THREE: 1

When the scene opens, Ma Ubu is on stage, alone in her armchair, although Niles is lying asleep on the table.

MA UBU: Another night alone at home. Is this a marriage?

The vulture puppet on a stick squawks, and the following text appears on the screen: **The game warder's wife wears a fur collar.**

MA UBU: Every night out with his dogs. No-one to dinner, and no invitations. It isn't normal. Old Ubu, what of the balls and concerts we used to know? Those were heroic days, so cosmopolitan. Now I sit in the silent darkness, and wait for his return. If I could only find some proof of Pa's whoring, I'd take him to court and grind 'til his pockets bled gold.

Ma Ubu climbs off the armchair. She begins to search about the room.

MA UBU: Where will I find the charms and letters?

She begins to exit. At this point, Niles, who is still sleeping on the bed, whines in his sleep, moves a bit, whimpers. This catches Ma Ubu's attention.

MA UBU: And what gives you uneasy dreams and such a full belly? Here my lovely, come to Mama.

She draws Niles toward her, against her breasts.

NILES: Here, watch your fingers, old girl.

MA UBU: But Niles, I only want to see what lies he's been feeding you.

NILES: Well, perhaps in the scheme of things, you're one of the ones who Needs to Know.

ACT THREE: 2

Ma Ubu opens Niles' handles, tipping out the contents that Pa Ubu had stuffed into him. A stack of crumpled papers and rags comes out of him. These are all bits and pieces of evidence, document, of Pa Ubu's political-criminal activities. As Ma Ubu spreads these out, piece by piece, images fill the screen and sounds fill the auditorium.

At two distinct points in this sequence, Pa Ubu emerges on stage, to partici-pate in the revelation. He speaks in Afrikaans, while Ma Ubu translates his words into English.

PA UBU AS PERPETRATOR: **Ons het dit 'tubing' genoem.**

MA UBU: We called it 'tubing'.

Ons vat 'n binneband en trek dit oor die gesig van die gevangene.
We would take an inner tube, and put it over the face of the detainee.

Ons sny 'n spleet in die binneband vir die tong.
We cut a slit in the tube for the tongue.

Dis hoe ons die waarheid kry.
This is how we got the truth.

Ons wurg hom, totdat hy iets het om to vertel.
We would suffocate him, until he had something to tell us.

Aan die lengte van die tong kan ons aflei hoe naby hy aan versmor-ing is.
From the length of the tongue we could tell how close he was to asphyxiation.

Ook as sy broek nat word, dan weet jy hy staan by die Pearly Gates.
Also, when he wet his pants, you knew he was standing at the Pearly Gates.

As hulle nog steeds weier om te praat
If they still refused to talk

Het ons hulle doodgeslaan met ysterpype wat in die plaasstoor gele het.
We beat them to death with iron pipes which we found in the farm-house.

Dit het ons in Cradock gedoen.
This we did in Cradock.

Finally, Pa Ubu makes the following statement in English.

PA UBU: They put the makarov pistol to the top of his head and pulled the trigger. The gun jammed. We got another gun from one of the

askaris. That didn't work either, so in the end we beat him to death with a spade. Then we each grabbed a hand and a foot, and put the body on the pyre of tyre and wood, poured petrol on it, and set it alight. Now of course, the burning of a body to ashes takes about seven hours; it is—ah—and—ah—whilst that happened we were drinking and even having a braai next to the fire.

At the end of the sequence of evidence, we return to Ma Ubu.

MA UBU: *(Weeping)* The sly old jackal. I had no idea Pa was so important! All along, I thought he was betraying me and here he was, hard at work, protecting me from the Swart Gevaar. *(Wipes her eyes sentimentally. Change of mood.)* Still, this is my chance. A girl can't be too careful! Who can she turn to once her charms begin to fade? While the overstuffed dummy is out of the way, I will seize this little stash of daring tales and sell them, to secure my old age, which is of course a long way off.

She grabs her handbag by the handles and exits.

Lights out.

ACT FOUR: 1

Pa Ubu enters.

PA UBU: MAAAAA! We are thirsty.

Silence.

PA UBU: MAAAAA! We are hungry.

Silence.

PA UBU: MAAAAA! We are being ignored!!

Silence.

PA UBU: Now where is the woman? She knows she's not allowed to go out when I might want her. Ma? … Mama? … Little Mommy? Boo hoo. We are abandoned, orphaned at the tender age of forty-seven. All

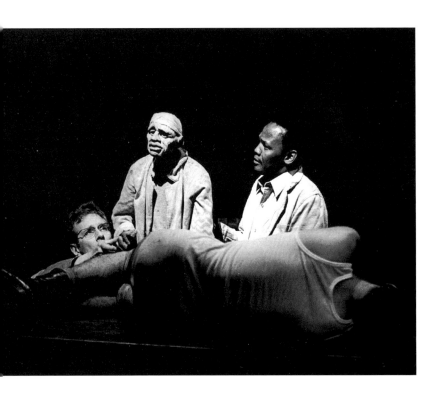

As Pa Ubu sleeps a witness puppet
appears, as if in a dream, to stand
over Pa Ubu's body. The witness tells
the story of the death of his child. The
sleeping torso at times seems to
become the figure of the dead child
described in the witness puppet's testimony. However, as Pa Ubu twitches
and moans in his sleep, we are
reminded that this is the body of the
recumbent dreamer.

alone. WE ARE ALONE. Only the empty arms of the night around us. Night night. Mama, come home.

Pa Ubu curls up in a foetal position. He takes out his music box which, as he turns the handle, plays 'Nkosi Sikelel'iAfrika'. As Pa Ubu goes to sleep, he dreams.

ACT FOUR: 2

While he sleeps, Pa Ubu has tormented dreams. These are suggested through animation on screen. A small tripod figure dances above Pa Ubu's head, stabbing at him with his spiked limbs. The puppet who had a Spaza shop at the Ubu dining-table appears, and takes up his position standing behind the body of the sleeping Pa Ubu. He presents the following testimony:

CAPTION ON SCREEN: *A Scholar's Tale*.

WITNESS: **Lomlungu wesikhafu esibomuu, wadubula lomntwana ngompu.**
This white man with a red scarf, he shot at the child with his rifle.

Ndambona eruqa umntwana wam u Scholar.
I saw him dragging my child, Scholar.

U Scholar wayeseswekekile.
Scholar was already dead.

Wayemtsala ngemilenze njengenja njengenja ecunyuzwe endleleni.
He was dragging him by the legs, like a dog, like a dog that is crushed in the road.

Ndambona esimba umgodi wokufaka ubuchopo buka Scholar.
I saw him digging a hole—for Scholar's brains—

Ilanga lalithe nka kodwa suke kwabamnyama xa ndimbona elele apho eli linxeba elingasoze liphele.
The sun was bright but it went dark when I saw him lying there. It's an everlasting pain.

Andiqondi ukuba iyakuze iphele entliziyweni yam.
I do not think that it will ever stop in my heart.

These four stills are taken from
Ma Ubu's TV interview, and
should be imagined as vast and
disembodied, projected onto the
screen behind the stage. See the
photograph on page 50.

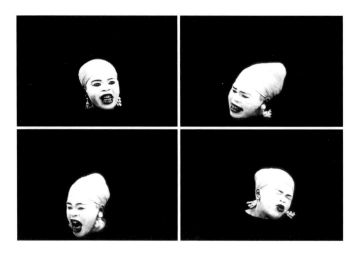

Babephethe abantu okwe zilwanyana yiyo lento endenza ndikhale kungoku,
They were treating people like animals ... that's what makes me cry right now,

nokuba sekuyinja, awuyibulali ngoluhlob,
... even a dog ... you don't kill it like that,

noba yimbovane, inmobane encinci,
even an ant, a small little ant,

uba novelwano ngembovane,
you have feelings for an ant,

kodwa ngoku, abantwana bethu, babengathathwa nanjengembovane.
but now, our children, they were not even taken as ants.

Pa Ubu writhes as he sleeps. Finally, he wakes up, and stares before him.

ACT FOUR: 3

Pa Ubu wakes from his dream to see Ma Ubu's head in an animation on the screen. She is in mid-interview, as if on a giant TV screen.

SCREEN MA: *(To TV interviewer)* Oh no. He was very polite, and such a good dancer. We called him the Nijinsky of Nylstroom.

PA UBU: What the bloody hell's going on here?

SCREEN MA: Mind you, he wasn't a homo, if you know what I mean.

PA UBU: Who said I was?

SCREEN MA: Always over weekends, he'd go fishing with the guys. He was a man's man. Although he was also a bit of a lady's man.

PA UBU: What do you think you're saying?

SCREEN MA: *(She frowns down at him, irritated.)* He was proud, you know, took care of himself.

PA UBU: Old sow, what are you doing?

SCREEN MA: *(Ignoring him)* He had a creative side, too. Always doing things with his hands.

PA UBU: Thula, phela khula! *(Ma Ubu notices Pa Ubu. He tries to turn her off with the remote control for the TV.)*

SCREEN MA: *(To TV interviewer)* He spoke Xhosa before he spoke English. He could always communicate with the garden boys. Oooh, how he loved the weight of a spade in his hand.

PA UBU: Wait a bit—where's this going now? Mother, we will debrain you, if you don't stop babbling. And if we can't find your brain, we will cut your head off.

SCREEN MA: His favourite meal? *(She hums, trying to recollect.)*

PA UBU: Meat, you old cow.

SCREEN MA: *(As if recollecting)* It was meat—he always liked his meat. A nice steak, with a monkey-gland sauce. He liked to drink—

PA UBU: I'm no bloody alcoholic!

SCREEN MA: —but I never saw him drunk.

PA UBU: HEY!

SCREEN MA: He could hold his liquor.

PA UBU: HEY!—Hey, hey, hey!!!!

SCREEN MA: *(Aside to Pa Ubu)* Hey! Ndidikwe yilembaxo uyenzayo wena, kunini uphoxana phakathi kwabantu![1]
(To TV interviewer) If he has a fault, I'd have to say that he is too loyal.

PA UBU: What would you know about loyalty, you traitor!

SCREEN MA: *(Aside, to Pa Ubu)* Yintoni ozokuyenza olokuqala nje, ufunantoni apha?[2]
(To TV interviewer) When I discovered what he had been doing all these years, you could have knocked me down with a feather.

PA UBU: What are you talking about?

SCREEN MA: I have maps, and plans, and names, important names.

PA UBU: Madam! Those are official secrets.

SCREEN MA: And cheque books, and films, and tapes, and so many things. He knew everyone.

Here the large Ubu figure which we have seen on the projection screen appears as a life-size, three-dimensional body puppet. See Act Four: 4.

PA UBU: If I go down, you do down with me!

SCREEN MA: *(Screaming at Pa Ubu)* Kutheni lento uzokuphoxisa ngam phakathi kwabantu abaninzi kangaka? Uyaintoyokuba, mna, njengoba ndilapha nje ndize ngenxa yoba ndizokwenza umabonakude. Ngoku uzokuphoxisa ngam phakathi abazinzi kangaka. Yhu! Uqaqadekile yaz'ba uqaqadekile. Yaz'ba bendingakwazi uba uqatsele kangaka. Yhu! Awusoze undiphoxe mna andiphoxakali kalulu. Ukrwada into oqale ngayo. Ufuzile ufuz'unyoko ngobukrwada obungaka.[3]

PA UBU: *(Screaming at Ma Ubu)* Jou dom ding—wat die vok doen jy? Jy het ons al twee vermoor—weet jy nie wat angaan nie? Wie die donner dink jy is ek? Ek gaan jou slaan teen die muur totdat jou tande uitval, jou blerrie stuk biltong. Kom, kom. Ek sal vir jou wys, wat is 'n man! Kom! Jou Ma se gat![4]

SCREEN MA: *(Back to TV interviewer)* No, we haven't actually signed any contracts yet, but we've got some things in the pipeline.

At this point, Pa Ubu mutes Ma Ubu on screen with the TV remote.

PA UBU: I can't believe it. I know that we should be sceptical of phenomena witnessed in the televisual media—but Ma *(gesturing toward the screen)*—she's turned us in! Sold us out! Buggered us up! Struck us down. There she is, selling our secrets to the highest bidder. You stupid cuttlefish! Just wait 'til I get you back home! Remember the sjambok, Ma.

ACT FOUR: 4

Toyi-toying music is heard in the background. The large Pa Ubu shadow figure enters.

PA UBU: W—w—who's there?

SHADOW: We've met before.
In times of war.

PA UBU: Oh, it's you again.

SHADOW: I'm here with some advice. Would it be correct to say, that at

present you've considered only two options: conceal or reveal?

PA UBU: How economically expressed.

SHADOW: I have another suggestion: shift the burden of guilt. Take the initiative; find a name, and remove yourself from all trace of blame. Extract yourself from the plot of your own history.

PA UBU: We have nothing to be ashamed of. We were only doing our job!

A puppeteer enters with a witness puppet.

WITNESS: **Indlela abambulala ngayo unyana wam, bemntitha edongeni, saza samfumana enentloko edumbileyo,**
The way they killed my son, hitting him against a wall, and we found him with a swollen head,

bambulala ngolunya andiqondi ukuba ndingaze ndixole kwelityala,
they killed him in a tragic manner and I don't think I'll ever forgive, in this case,

ngakumbi lamapolisa enza lento nala ayekhona.
especially the police who were involved and who were there.

Andiqondi ukuba noba ndingabekwa ukuba ndibe ngumsebenzi emakhitshini ukuba ndingadlisa ityhefu abantwana babelungu.
I wouldn't think anything, if ever I was to be brought as a maid, if I were to poison these white men's children.

PA UBU: It wasn't personal. It was war!

This puppet exits. Another enters.

WITNESS: **Ba ne sa utlwisa bonna jwa me botlhoko ka motlakase.**
They electrocuted my private parts.

Mongwe wa bona o ne a gotetsa motlakatse.
The one switched on the switch.

O mongwe o ne a gatelletse go botsa 'A oa batla go re bolella gore Edwin a kae?'
The other one kept on asking, 'Do you want to tell us where Edwin is?'

Kgapetsa kgapetsa ke ne ke babollela gore ga ke itse kwa a leng teng.
I kept on telling them I didn't know where he was.

O mongwe o ne a tshwere bontlha bongwe ba toulo mme o mongwe a tshwere bo bongwe.
They also strangled me with a towel.

Bobedi ba bone ba e goga ka thata.
The one was holding one end of the towel, the other was holding the other end, and each one was pulling.

Ke a itse gore ke bo mang banna ba badirileng se mo gonna.
I know who these men are who did this to me.

PA UBU: Communists!!! *(Shouting at the puppet)*

SHADOW: These voices will be heard. Ignore me at your peril.

The Shadow disappears. Pa Ubu is left alone. There should be a momentary sense of his bewilderment. Then he recovers himself.

PA UBU: Perhaps the old man had a point after all. I begin to feel the pitchfork prodding my arse.

ACT FOUR: 5

Pa Ubu picks up his lavatory brush, looks into it as a mirror. He scrutinizes his face; squeezes pimples. This triggers a sequence of animations on screen, which coincide with Pa Ubu on stage decoding his own body, using the toilet-brush as a kind of Geiger counter. Pa Ubu clears his throat, straightens an invisible tie, poses, rehearses as if preparing to make a formal statement:

PA UBU: There's one thing that I will have to live with until the day I die—it's the corpses that I have to drag with me to my grave, of the people I have killed. Remorse, I can assure you, a lot, a hell of a lot.

He looks up.

PA UBU: Now that we have seen what we are made of, it seems that we have very few options. We will have to get Brutus to join our submission; then we'll blame all on politics and beguile the Commission.

The vulture puppet on a stick squawks, and the following text appears on the screen: **High tide may vary, but low tide finds its mark.**

PA UBU: Here Brutus! Here boys. *(He whistles Pa Ubu's whistle)*

The dogs come lolloping onto the stage.

HEAD ONE: How can we serve?

HEAD TWO: How may we flatter?

HEAD THREE: Who's head is wanted on a platter?

PA UBU: Boys, you'll have to clean up your act—we're going into show business.

The dogs begin to snarl.

HEAD ONE: Not so fast, old Ubu. It occurs to me that what you have in mind is the 'show-and-tell' business.

HEAD TWO: We hate to disagree with you, boss, but we've discussed this option, and have decided that we're better off biting our tongues.

HEAD THREE: After all, what's there to link us with any of it? Not a paw-print anywhere.

HEAD TWO: They don't have a single bone to pick with us.

At this quip, the dogs laugh inanely together.

HEAD ONE: We respectfully advise you to follow us, master. A split in our ranks could hasten disaster.

HEAD TWO: We'd deeply regret any signs of dissent.

HEAD THREE: A collusion of silence is our joint intent.

HEAD TWO: That's it! Keep quiet, lie low, and in a year or two we'll all have our old jobs back.

PA UBU: Yes, yes. No doubt you're right. We must all stick together.

At this point Pa Ubu and the dogs break into a song routine:

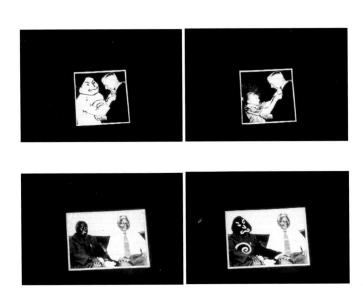

SONG

PA UBU: Old Brutus here has said it's one for all

CHORUS OF HEADS: It's one for all

PA UBU: He'd persuade me that we stand as one or fall

CHORUS: Until we fall

PA UBU: A pact of silence these three dogs and I now jointly share

CHORUS: The joints we share

PA UBU: Our acts of violence are too awful for us to declare

CHORUS: The awful we declare

PA UBU: We claim extenuation from post-traumatic stress disorder

CHORUS: We stress disorder

PA UBU: We'll avoid the pious call, as we've put Tu and Tu together

CHORUS: Tu Tu Tu Tu

PA UBU: The Archbishop's plans may promise rainbows, but for us its heavy weather.

CHORUS: Tu Tu Tu Tu.

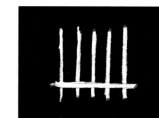

An idea dawns. While the dogs sing a jazz routine, Pa Ubu tiptoes out, returns with documents. As the dogs finish their song, they fall asleep. Pa Ubu gingerly opens Brutus's suitcase belly, fills the belly with the evidence.

PA UBU: *(Front of stage.)* Good, we've hopefully muzzled our dogs. Now to cover them in dirt before we send them to the cleaners.

Pa Ubu goes to a drawer and takes out his old photograph album. He begins to page through it, rearranging images.

Pa Ubu sneaks off stage. On the screen, the image of the three dog-bowls with neck-cuffs, sounds of the dogs howling.

ACT FIVE: 1

In the following scene, we have the sentencing of Brutus.

JUDGE: In the matter of the state versus Brutus, Brutus, and Brutus: it has been determined that there is unequal culpability, and we thus hand down, separately, three distinct sentences.

With regard to the first case: a head of political affairs cannot always foresee how his vision will be implemented. We thus exonerate you, and retire you with full pension.

With regard to the head of the military: there is no evidence to link you directly to these barbarous acts. Nonetheless, an example must be made of you, or who knows where we'll end up. You are thus sentenced to thirty years in the leadership of the new state army.

Finally, to the dog who allowed himself to become the agent of these ghastly deeds: you have been identified by the families of victims; you have left traces of your activities everywhere. We thus sentence you to two hundred and twelve years imprisonment.

As the sentences are handed down, the dogs react:

HEAD THREE: This judgement is a sham.

HEAD TWO: We're all being tarred with the same brush.

HEAD THREE: Amnesty! We appeal for amnesty! Let us come before the Truth Commission. We have other stories to tell!

HEADS TWO AND THREE: Yes, we have stories, oooh, what we could tell you! Let us speak!

Lights out.

On screen, we see a drawing of prison bars. Brutus remains on stage, the bars on screen behind him.

ACT FIVE: 2

Pa Ubu enters. He addresses the audience.

PA UBU: A good lawyer can be a skeleton key, but it seems that Brutus's judge was a deadbolt who would lock him away forever. We can't say we blame him for looking for amnesty. But the truth is, some of his

The **SMELL** ↙

of BLOOD and **DYNAMITE**

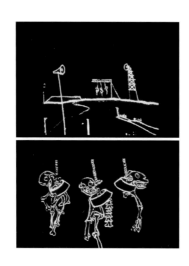

stories might cast us as lead. Our only solution is to cast him in lead.

There is the clanging of metal doors and the sounds of footsteps approaching. It is evident that we are in the prison. As Ubu approaches, the dogs start sniffing.

CAPTION ON SCREEN: ***The Smell of Blood and Dynamite***

HEAD ONE: I know that smell!

Pa Ubu enters. The dogs whimper and whine at his arrival. Pa Ubu makes hushing gestures. He leads the dogs off.

PA UBU: *(To audience)* As my father always said, if you want something done properly, you've got to do it yourself. And clean up afterwards.

Lights off on stage. Image of hanged dogs on screen.

ACT FIVE: 3

On screen, images of tripod-figures rushing back and forth. Ma Ubu enters. She struts into centre stage, waving her hand to invisible crowds. At the same time, Pa Ubu strides purposefully onto stage, a file of papers under his arm. They bump into each other at centre stage.

MA UBU: Oh! ahhh—umm. Good Day, Pa.

PA UBU: She greets me! The two-faced sow greets me! *(Murderously, under his breath)* Curse you, Madam, for your betrayal. A wife is such a nuisance that we resolve never to marry. Only now it's too late, because we are already married, and thus you have made a liar of us and we are entitled to bash you.

MA UBU: What are you going on about, you great bladder?

PA UBU: You've stolen our best defence, which was the record of our offence. We have nothing left to bargain with.

MA UBU: But Pa, I did it for us.

PA UBU: Do you think we were born yesterday? You did it for yourself. My father always said never trust a woman unless you can fill her purse.

UBU **Tells the TRUTH**

MA UBU: He wasn't talking about money, Pa! But what do you know of a woman's needs?

PA UBU: We know they need to be beaten and then scrambled.

MA UBU: No, stinkpot, not any more. I won't take it. No more threats. I have too much on you.

PA UBU: Not as much as you might think, Ma. It's a question of who you know, not just of who we knew. We've washed our hands so clean, they're almost spotless.

VOICE OVER MICROPHONE: Will the next witness to testify please come forward. Mister … Ubu?

ACT FIVE: 4

CAPTION ON SCREEN: *Ubu Tells The Truth*

Pa Ubu steps up to the podium. He taps one of the microphones: hollow echoing tapping noise, feedback. Pa Ubu steps forward to speak. A spotlight comes up on him.

PA UBU: I stand before you with neither shame nor arrogance. I am not a monster. I am an honest citizen, and would never break the law. Like all of you, I eat, and sleep, and dream dreams. These vile stories, they sicken me. When I am told of what happened here, I cannot believe it. These things, they were done by those above me; those below me; those beside me. I too have been betrayed! I knew nothing.

There is a shift in performance style here, which is marked also by the shift from 'I' back to 'we' in Pa Ubu's speech. At the same time, the microphones, which are puppets controlled from below the podium, begin to move about, taunting and mocking Pa Ubu, avoiding his grasp.

PA UBU: I love my family. But their future was being stolen from them. Our destiny used to be in our own hands. Then the international conspiracies against us cut off our arms. Where could we go, we other Africans? Our children became the servants of servants, with their bowing, and vowing, and scraping, and it was left to our corpulent self to do the whipping, and stripping, and raping. Such loyalty is no longer fashionable, except in some smaller countries. But how is an

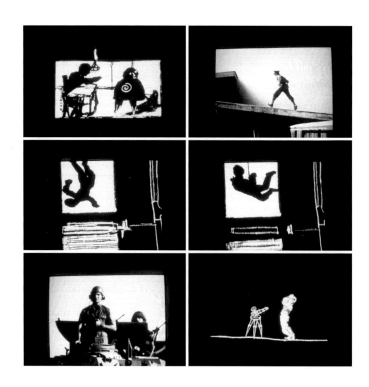

army to survive if it will not reward in public what it knows is done in secret? I tell you, I served in bloody … I served in bloody … I served in bloody good units. And I'm proud to have served with them. Soldiering is not a selfish profession, as a true soldier is prepared to lay down his life for his fellow citizens and for his country. THIS IS MY COUNTRY. And I won't give it away without a damn good fight.

Pa Ubu finally, in frustration, seizes a microphone in his hand. He now makes a very still and formal statement, the one which we have heard him rehearse earlier.

PA UBU: There's only one thing I will have to live with until the day I die—it's the corpses that I will have to drag with me to my grave, of the people I have killed. Remorse, I can assure you, a lot, a hell of a lot.

Pa Ubu sings his hymn.

PA UBU's HYMN: How dark is my day at noon, Oh God,
How unjust the sins that I bear
Despite all the dangerous paths that I trod
To save my own people despair.

CHORUS: O the blood, O the blood,
O the blood of the lamb sets me free
Send a flood, send a flood
Send your blood like a flood over me.

And then I recall another dark day
When you hung on the arms of the cross,
You carried all our vile deeds away
And burned up our past sins as dross.

CHORUS: O the blood, O the blood,
O the blood of the lamb sets me free
Send a flood, send a flood
Send your blood like a flood over me.

Throughout the hymn, there are images from the evidence sequence on screen.

As his hymn concludes, the fullbodied voice of a massed chorus singing 'Nkosi' swells and fills the auditorium, and crowds are projected on the screen. Pa Ubu finally freezes, unable to compete with the masses projected around him in image

As Pa Ubu sings his hymn, the screen is filled with images from archival film documenting a spontaneous public celebration following the unbanning of the African National Congress.

and song. He is wheeled off stage on his lectern, as if he is a statue being removed.

Lights out.

ACT FIVE: 5

Ma Ubu and Pa Ubu on a boat. The vulture is with them, as is Ma Ubu's kitty.

MA UBU: What a lovely breeze!

PA UBU: We are moving at an almost miraculous speed. I say, our mother, the wind is rather refreshing. I hope we don't capsize!

MA UBU: Hoist the mainsail. Man the jib. *(Doing nothing)*

PA UBU: Close haul the mizzen mast. *(Doing nothing)*

MA UBU: See, Pa, how well we can manage if we just stick together. How much further is it?

PA UBU: *(Looking down a telescope)* By my computations, about half an hour. Not much more, anyway, than two or three days; ten months at the absolute outside.

MA UBU: I say, Pa, what's that bobbing in the water?

At this, Niles swims into view, following the boat.

NILES: Ahoy there, Captain, what a fine day. Looks like there'll be plain sailing ahead. Would there be room for me on board?

PA UBU: Niles! Old friend! How unlikely to see you here, in the Sargasso. Climb in!

Niles clambers aboard.

PA UBU: Well now, this is more like it. Three's a Company . . .

NILES: As old Brutus always used to say.

PA UBU: Er, yes, well, quite.

MA UBU: I'm going to miss all the old friends. Still, enough of the past.

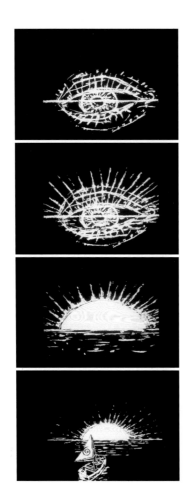

What we need is a fresh start.

NILES: A clean slate.

MA UBU: A new beginning.

PA UBU: A bright future.

*The vulture puppet on a stick flaps his wings repeatedly and squawks. The following text appears on the screen: **My slice of old cheese and your loaf of fresh bread will make a tolerable meal.***

This text is replaced by an image of Ma Ubu and Pa Ubu's boat floating on a sea, towards the giant eye. The eye turns into a setting sun, as the boat floats off toward the horizon.

Lights out.

Endnotes:

1   Hey! I'm sick and tired of this nonsense. How long have you been degrading me in front of people?
2   What are you doing here in the first place? What do you want hey?
3   Why are you belittling me in front of all these people? Do you know my reason for being here is to be interviewed on television? And now you're mocking me in front of all these people. You are a pest, a bloody pest! I wasn't aware you were such a nuisance. You are never going to make a fool of me. That doesn't happen easily. You're so rude. You have inherited this rudeness from your mother.
4   You stupid thing—what the fuck are you doing? You've killed us—don't you know what is going on? Who the hell do you think I am? I'm going to knock you against the wall so hard your teeth will fall out. You bloody piece of biltong. Come on—I'll show you who's a man! Come on! Your mother's arse ...!